IT'S TIME TO LEARN ABOUT CROCODILES

It's Time to Learn about Crocodiles

Walter the Educator

Silent King Books
A WhichHead Entertainment Imprint

Copyright © 2025 by Walter the Educator

All rights reserved. No part of this book may be reproduced in any manner whatsoever without written per- mission except in the case of brief quotations embodied in critical articles and reviews.

First Printing, 2024

Disclaimer

This book is a literary work; the story is not about specific persons, locations, situations, and/or circumstances unless mentioned in a historical context. Any resemblance to real persons, locations, situations, and/or circumstances is coincidental. This book is for entertainment and informational purposes only. The author and publisher offer this information without warranties expressed or implied. No matter the grounds, neither the author nor the publisher will be accountable for any losses, injuries, or other damages caused by the reader's use of this book. The use of this book acknowledges an understanding and acceptance of this disclaimer.

It's Time to Learn about Crocodiles is a collectible early learning book by Walter the Educator suitable for all ages belonging to Walter the Educator's Collectible Early Learning Book Series. Collect more books at WaltertheEducator.com

USE THE EXTRA SPACE TO TAKE NOTES AND DOCUMENT YOUR MEMORIES

CROCODILES

Down by the river, deep and wide,

It's Time to Learn about
Crocodiles

Lives a reptile who likes to hide.

With scaly skin and toothy smile,

Say hello to the crocodile!

He's long and strong with armored back,

His color's green or sometimes black.

He glides through water, smooth and slow,

But on the land, he's quick to go!

His teeth are sharp, they number lots,

They help him chomp his food in spots.

Fish and frogs and birds he'll seek

He doesn't chew, just swallows sleek!

He's got a tail that's thick and stout,

It helps him swim and move about.

He swishes left, he swishes right,

With power strong and out of sight!

It's Time to Learn about
Crocodiles

His eyes are high upon his head,

They peek out while he stays in bed

A bed of water, calm and wide,

Where he can watch and still can hide.

His nose and ears are clever too,

They close up tight when diving through.

He holds his breath for quite a while,

What a skillful crocodile!

He lays her eggs on sandy shore,

And guards them well, and watches more.

When babies hatch, they make a peep,

And Mama helps them take a leap!

Though crocodiles may look so mean,

They're part of nature's balance scene.

They keep the rivers clean and neat,

It's Time to Learn about
Crocodiles

By munching things we'd never eat.

But keep your distance, that's the rule,

Don't treat a croc like it's a tool.

They're wild and strong, they like their space

So give them time and give them grace.

Now you know this reptile's style,

The sneaky, swimming crocodile.

With toothy grin and clever eyes,

It's Time to Learn about Crocodiles

He lives beneath the sunny skies!

ABOUT THE CREATOR

Walter the Educator is one of the pseudonyms for Walter Anderson. Formally educated in Chemistry, Business, and Education, he is an educator, an author, a diverse entrepreneur, and he is the son of a disabled war veteran. "Walter the Educator" shares his time between educating and creating. He holds interests and owns several creative projects that entertain, enlighten, enhance, and educate, hoping to inspire and motivate you. Follow, find new works, and stay up to date with Walter the Educator™

at WaltertheEducator.com

www.ingramcontent.com/pod-product-compliance
Lightning Source LLC
LaVergne TN
LVHW051920060526
838201LV00060B/4101